I0797603

▶ YouTubers

JAMES CHARLES

JESSICA RUSICK

Checkerboard Library
An Imprint of Abdo Publishing
abdobooks.com

abdobooks.com

Published by Abdo Publishing, a division of ABDO, PO Box 398166, Minneapolis, Minnesota 55439.

Printed in the United States of America, North Mankato, Minnesota
102019
012020

Design: Sarah DeYoung, Mighty Media, Inc.
Production: Mighty Media, Inc.
Editor: Rebecca Felix
Cover Photograph: Shutterstock Images
Interior Photographs: Alamy Stock Photo, p. 15; Charles Sykes/AP Images, p. 27; Eugene Gologursky/Getty Images, pp. 23 (top), 25, 29 (bottom); Mighty Media, Inc., p. 23 (bottom); Nancy Rivera/Bauer-Griffin/Getty Images, p. 19; Santiago Felipe/Getty Images, p. 13; Shutterstock Images, pp. 7, 9, 10, 23 (middle), 28; Stefanie Keenan/Getty Images, pp. 17, 21; Sthanlee B. Mirador/AP Images, p. 5; Tess_Trunk/iStockphoto, pp. 6, 14, 18, 20, 23, 26, 28, 29; Wikimedia Commons, pp. 11, 29 (top)

Library of Congress Control Number: 2019943324

Publisher's Cataloging-in-Publication Data
Names: Rusick, Jessica, author.
Title: James Charles / by Jessica Rusick
Description: Minneapolis, Minnesota : Abdo Publishing, 2020 | Series: YouTubers | Includes online resources and index.
Identifiers: ISBN 9781532191794 (lib. bdg.) | ISBN 9781644943571 (pbk.) | ISBN 9781532178528 (ebook)
Subjects: LCSH: Dickinson, James C. (James Charles)--Juvenile literature. | YouTube (Firm)--Juvenile literature. | Internet celebrities--Biography--Juvenile literature. | Cosmetics--Juvenile literature. | Internet videos--Juvenile literature. | Video blogs--Juvenile literature. | Internet entertainment industry--Juvenile literature.
Classification: DDC 646.72092--dc23

Contents

Check Out James Charles

James Charles is a YouTube star and beauty **vlogger**. He posts videos about makeup products and **techniques**. His YouTube channel has more than 15 million **subscribers**. James's videos have been viewed more than 1.5 billion times!

James was interested in makeup from a young age. But he did not experiment with wearing or applying it until his teenage years. Since then, James has become one of the top makeup artists on YouTube. His **tutorials** show viewers how to create bold, colorful looks.

More than anything, James uses makeup to promote **gender** equality. He believes makeup can make people of any gender feel **confident**. This belief has led James to break many social and cultural **barriers**. But he did not set out to do this. James simply followed his passion for beauty.

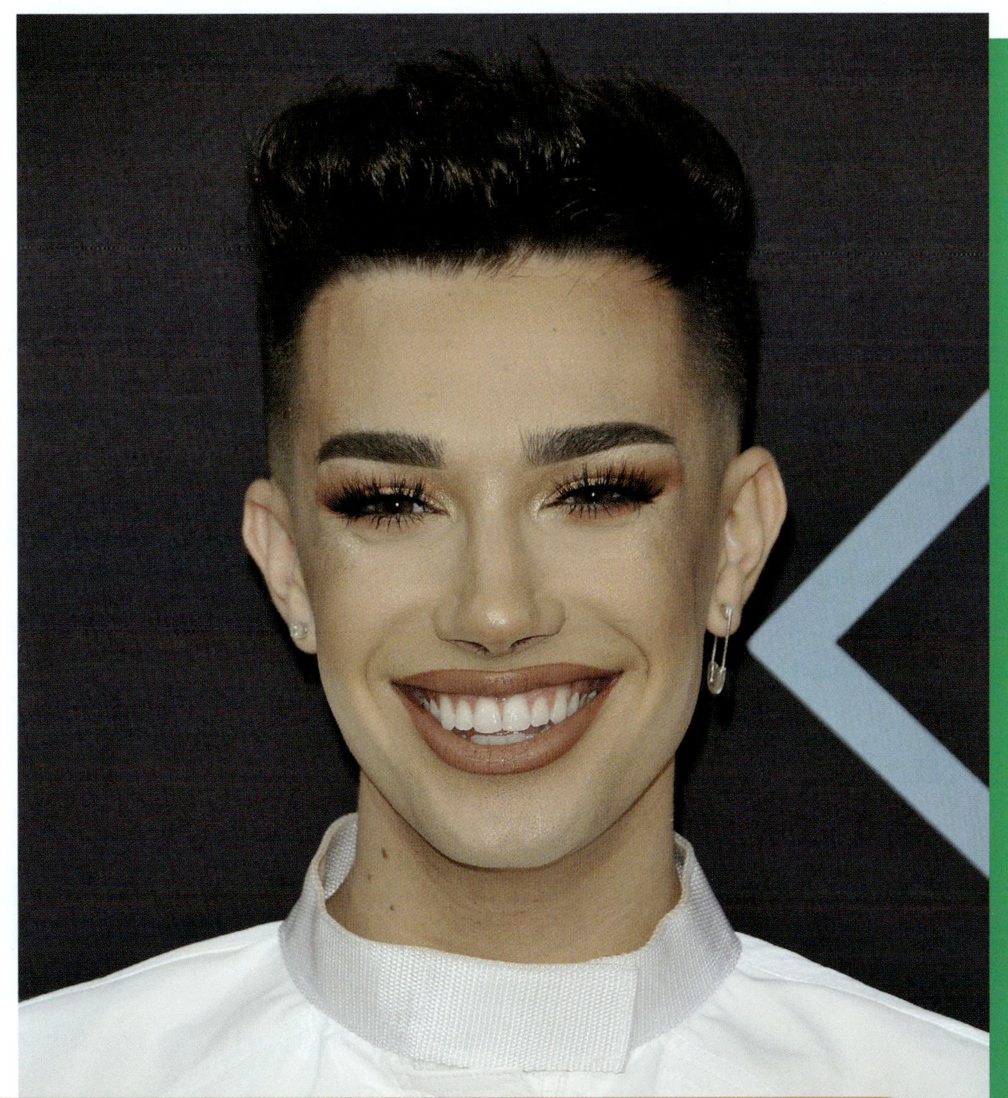

James Charles has inspired many people by staying true to himself and wearing makeup despite gender norms.

Young Stylist

James Charles Dickinson was born on May 23, 1999, in Bethlehem, New York. He is named after his two grandfathers, James and Charles. James's mom is Christine. His dad is Skip. James has one younger brother, Ian.

From a young age, James showed an interest in beauty and art. James loved to dress his brother in their mother's clothes and shoes. He also loved to draw.

James's father encouraged his son's **creativity**. When James was three years old, his father taught him how to braid hair. From then on, James liked to style hair whenever he could.

James styled the hair of Barbie dolls. And once, he even braided a friend's hair while they were both playing in a T-ball game!

James is legally blind. He wears special contact lenses to help him see! As long as he wears them, James says his condition does not affect his ability to do makeup.

When James was 12 years old, he came out to his parents as gay. James was concerned about how his parents would react. But his family was supportive.

James felt grateful to have his parents' support. He knew that coming out was a difficult experience for many gay people. The love and support James received from his family provided him a solid base to build a future.

Hair & Makeup

In 2013, James started school at Bethlehem Central High School. Here, he continued his artistic pursuits, including drawing. James's favorite thing to draw were faces of female celebrities. He used **charcoal** for these drawings. James also worked with paint.

James continued hairstyling too. Throughout high school, he often styled his friends' hair for fun and for special occasions. In 2015, James had just finished styling his friend's hair for an event when she realized she was late for a makeup appointment. So, she asked James if he could do her makeup as well.

At first, James was uncertain. For years, he had loved to watch YouTube makeup **tutorials**. In these videos, YouTube makeup artists show viewers how to apply makeup to create different looks. Though James had watched many tutorials, he had never tried to apply makeup on himself or anyone else. Still, he decided to help out his friend.

James soon discovered makeup brand favorites. In 2018, he said he rarely switches to new brands or products because his favorites work so well.

James applied his friend's makeup. And they were both happy with the result! His friend even posted a photo of her makeup look on the social media site Instagram.

Other people saw the Instagram photo and wanted James to do their makeup as well. So, James ordered a makeup kit online and started practicing his application skills. Soon, social media would take James's makeup game to a whole new level.

Instagram Artist

James's artistic talent made him a natural with makeup. And as he practiced his application skills, he became more **confident**. On August 29, 2015, James decided to start posting his makeup looks on Instagram.

At first, James photographed and posted makeup looks he created for his friends. Then on September 18, James posted his first makeup selfie on Instagram. For this photo, James wore a full face of skeleton makeup for Halloween. It was the first time he had ever worn makeup.

James discovered that he liked wearing makeup. From then on, most of his Instagram photos of makeup looks featured himself.

In 2019, James had more than 700 posts on his Instagram account.

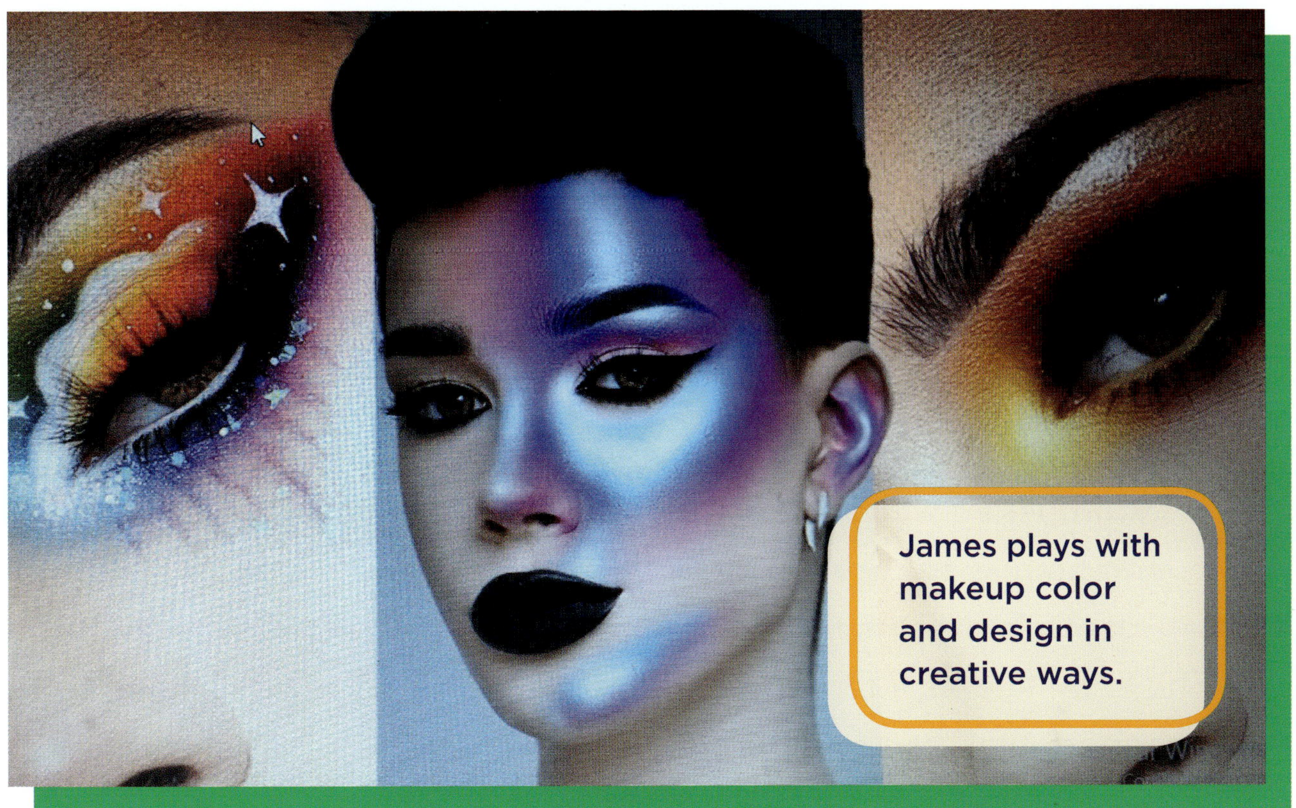

James plays with makeup color and design in creative ways.

Many of James's makeup looks used bold eyeshadows, dark lipsticks, and fake freckles. James also became known for his use of highlighter. This is face makeup that attracts light. James often applied highlighter to his cheekbones and nose. This gave his face a soft, **subtle** glow.

James posted both inventive and everyday makeup looks. In one October post, he used makeup to make himself look like a character from a comic book!

Discord & Debut

James's Instagram account quickly gained a following. By November 2015, he had more than 5,000 **subscribers**! But as James's online success took off, he hit what he called a "rough patch" with his family. His parents felt uncertain about James's new passion for wearing makeup.

James's parents thought James wore makeup because he identified as a female. But James explained that he was comfortable with his male **gender** identity. Wearing makeup was simply a way for him to express his artistic talent. And one day, he wanted to turn his talent into a career.

It took time for James's parents to understand this. But they remained supportive. James's father even helped James build a makeup studio in their basement! It had a desk, a mirror lined with lights, and storage. James began shooting many of his Instagram photos there.

James does not identify as female. But he has dressed as the opposite sex for certain events and occasions.

Soon, James's fans wanted more than just photos. On Instagram, James only showed pictures of his finished makeup looks. His fans wanted to know the steps James took to create the looks.

On February 7, 2016, James posted his first makeup **tutorial** on Instagram. The short video received thousands of views, likes, and comments from James's growing fanbase. That month, he reached 100,000 Instagram **subscribers**!

James's fans wanted more tutorials from him. However, Instagram only allowed users to post one-minute-long videos. James wanted to create longer, more detailed tutorials. So, he created a YouTube channel, which allows hours-long videos.

James made his YouTube **debut** on March 3, 2016. He posted a makeup tutorial video for a look he called "the serpent." James showed viewers all the steps he took to create this look.

James often stayed up late to create his makeup looks after school and work. James's dad often stayed up late too. So when James created a makeup look, he would ask his dad for feedback before posting a photo of it on Instagram.

Though many of James's posts feature inventive makeup looks, he often chooses more classic looks at events.

The video was a hit! James posted two more **tutorials**, on March 15 and March 17. By this time, his YouTube channel had 10,000 **subscribers**.

James continued to post on Instagram. But he was a rising YouTube star. And James's makeup passion also made him the face of a growing movement.

Makeup Movement

In May 2016, the fashion magazine *Marie Claire* featured James as an up-and-coming male beauty **vlogger**. James's interest in makeup made him part of a larger trend. More than ever, male social media stars were posting makeup looks.

Society often expects people to dress and behave in ways specific to their **genders**. These are called gender roles or gender stereotypes. Traditionally, females have been the main gender to wear makeup in Western culture. Many people felt it was not normal for males to wear makeup. James wanted to change this.

James wanted to help normalize wearing makeup for everyone. In the months following his *Marie Claire* feature, James continued to break **barriers**.

On September 6, 2016, James posted reshoots of his high school yearbook photos. He thought the lighting in the original photos made them look bad. So, he had the photos retaken. James said he brought his own light to the reshoots! This was to make the highlighter on his face stand out.

James (*right*) and Manny Gutierrez, who is known as Manny MUA on social media. Manny is a fellow male beauty vlogger helping break gender barriers in the beauty industry.

James's photos went **viral**. People shared them across social media. James and his senior photos also caught the attention of major makeup brand CoverGirl.

CoverGirl felt James was a role model. His posts helped make it more acceptable for anyone who wanted to wear makeup to do so. In October, the brand made James a CoverGirl spokesmodel. As a spokesmodel, James would appear in CoverGirl ads. He was the first male to fill this role!

Later that month, James appeared in ads for CoverGirl's new mascara So Lashy. This mascara was made for all lash types. So, it promoted "lash equality," just like James promoted **gender** and makeup equality! James was proud to be the face of a campaign focused on **inclusivity**.

James's high school photos caught the attention of celebrities. On Twitter, the actress Zendaya retweeted James and said, "You win!"

The mascara ad was one of many James did for CoverGirl over the next year. Balancing this work, his social media posts, and school was sometimes difficult for James. As his high school graduation neared, he thought more about his future in makeup.

James took part in Pride festivals in June 2019. These events celebrate LGBTQ persons and focus on inclusivity.

Los Angeles Living

In June 2017, James graduated high school. He wanted to continue his career in makeup. So, he moved to Los Angeles, California. This city is a hub of the entertainment industry and home to many famous makeup artists.

At first, living in a big city was not always easy for James. He came from a small town. So, he sometimes felt unsafe living in a more populated area. But James had friends in Los Angeles before he even moved there! One was beauty **vlogger** Tati Westbrook.

Westbrook had been posting makeup videos on YouTube since 2010. She was one of James's early makeup inspirations. James messaged Westbrook soon after his high

VIP Post

James sometimes applies makeup for celebrities. He has created makeup looks for reality TV and social media star Kylie Jenner, singer Iggy Azalea, and fellow YouTuber Liza Koshy!

school yearbook photos went **viral**, and the two became friends.

Westbrook became a **mentor** to James. As his YouTube stardom grew, Westbrook gave James advice and support.

James takes a selfie with media star Kim Kardashian West in 2017. Living in Los Angeles brought James many opportunities with celebrities.

By the end of 2017, the James Charles YouTube channel had grown massively. James had more than 2 million **subscribers** there! Viewers loved his makeup **tutorials**. But James had also begun posting other types of content.

YouTube Sensation

As James's YouTube fan base grew, so did his content. James still posted the makeup **tutorials** that made him famous. He also began posting makeup challenge videos.

In James's first challenge, he created a makeup look without using brushes to apply the makeup. Instead, he used his fingers to apply foundation, eyeshadow, and more. In another challenge, he applied his makeup without the use of a mirror.

Another new feature James created on his YouTube channel was a series called Beauty Battles. These videos feature James and two guests. Each guest puts makeup on one side of James's face. Then, James reviews their work and decides who did a better job applying the makeup!

James also posted what he called "chit chat get ready" videos. These videos feature makeup tutorials. But instead of discussing products and **techniques** during them, James shares stories from his past and answers fan questions. This let fans get to know James better.

New Channels

Makeup: In November 2018, James partnered with the makeup company Morphe to launch a makeup collection. It was called the Sister Collection.

Music: Since he was young, James has loved to sing. He is a member of an **a cappella** group called Flashback! The group has posted music covers on YouTube. One day, its members hope to make an album.

Clothing & Accessories: In 2017, James launched the Sisters Apparel line. It featured hooded sweatshirts and hats with funny sayings or the Sisters logo. In 2018, the line expanded to include pants, jackets, phone cases, and more.

James's new content along with his continual beauty **tutorials** made him more popular than ever. By May 2018, he had more than 5 million YouTube **subscribers**! And soon, James would **debut** even more new content.

Sister Squad

In the summer of 2018, James began posting a new type of video. It featured him and his friends who were fellow YouTube stars. This included twins Ethan and Grayson Dolan, who ran a popular comedy channel on YouTube. James became friends with the stars in 2017 after doing their makeup for Halloween!

YouTuber Emma Chamberlain joined the friend group in June 2018. Together, James, the Dolan twins, and Chamberlain formed the Sister Squad. This name came from James. He called his fans and friends "sisters."

The Sister Squad filmed YouTube videos together. On June 19, 2018, James posted the first Sister Squad video. In it, James gave Emma and the Dolan twins instructions on how to do their makeup. However, James and his friends were separated by a wall. So, he couldn't see what they were doing! Sister Squad videos became some of James's most popular.

In November 2018, James launched a new phase of his career. He partnered with the makeup company Morphe

The Sister Collection was promoted with the hashtag #UnleashYourInnerArtist.

to launch the Sister Collection. This makeup set featured a 39-shade rainbow eyeshadow palette, makeup brushes, and a beauty blending sponge.

The Sister Collection sold out the same day it **debuted**! This was the biggest sales day in Morphe's history. James was truly a star. But a **scandal** would soon disrupt his popularity.

Scandal & Resurgence

In spring 2019, James's YouTube career faced a setback. James had a public fight with his **mentor**, Westbrook. At first, many people sided with Westbrook and were upset with James. In May, James lost nearly 3 million YouTube **subscribers**.

On May 18, James shared his side of the story in the video "No More Lies." He and Westbrook said they would try to move on. Then James took a monthlong break from YouTube.

During James's break, his subscriber count slowly recovered. By June, he had gained back nearly 2 million subscribers. In a video posted that month, James told fans that taking time away from social media improved his mental state. However, James was happy to be back on YouTube. No matter what the future holds, James will continue following his passion sharing his makeup art with waiting fans.

VIP Post

"No More Lies" is the most popular video on James's YouTube channel. It has more than 40 million views.

James attends a May 2019 fashion event amidst his social media break. Upon returning to YouTube he told fans, “A sister is ready to get back to work!”

Timeline

1999

James Charles Dickinson is born on May 23 in Bethlehem, New York.

2011

James comes out to his parents as gay.

2013

James attends Bethlehem Central High School in Bethlehem, New York.

2015

James posts his first makeup selfie on Instagram.

2016

In March, James uploads his first YouTube video.

2016

In May, James is named an up-and-coming male beauty vlogger by *Marie Claire* magazine.

2016

James becomes CoverGirl's first male spokesmodel in October.

2018

In June, James forms the Sister Squad with the Dolan twins and Emma Chamberlain.

2019

In May, James has a public fight with his mentor, Tati Westbrook. James takes a monthlong break from YouTube.

2016

In September, James's high school yearbook photo post goes viral.

2017

James graduates high school. Soon after, he moves to Los Angeles.

2018

James launches the Sister Collection with makeup brand Morphe in November.

2019

James returns to YouTube in June.

Glossary

a cappella—without instrumental accompaniment.

barrier—a law or rule that makes something difficult or impossible.

charcoal—a black material that is a form of carbon.

confident—having faith in oneself and one's powers.

creativity—the quality of being imaginative and inventive.

debut (DAY-byoo)—a first appearance. To debut is to first appear or to present or perform something for the first time.

gender—the behaviors, characteristics, and qualities most often associated with either the male or female sex.

inclusivity—the quality of accepting and including all persons or groups.

mentor—a trusted advisor or guide.

scandal—an action that shocks people and disgraces those connected with it.

subscriber—someone who signs up to receive something on a regular basis.

subtle—difficult to perceive, or not obvious.

technique (tehk-NEEK)—a method or style in which something is done.

tutorial—a lesson on how to do something. Tutorials are often presented through media such as videos or computer programs.

viral—quickly or widely spread, usually by electronic communication.

vlog—a video log that tells about someone's personal opinions, activities, and experiences. A person who creates these logs is called a vlogger.

Online Resources

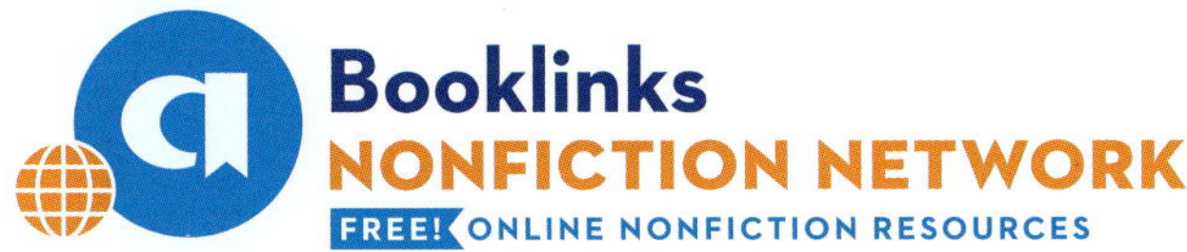

To learn more about James Charles, please visit **abdobooklinks.com** or scan this QR code. These links are routinely monitored and updated to provide the most current information available.

Index